Amazing

Theme-Based
ESL Worksheets for Beginners

THEME: COMMUNITY

✓ fun, photocopiable
✓ community places
✓ grammar & vocabulary activities
✓ games, listening & reading activities
✓ easy reading for low literacy levels

Baye Hunter

Hunter Publishing

Thank you to www.clker.com and www. http://office.microsoft.com/en-CA/images/ for use of domain free clipart.

First edition.

ISBN: 978-0991764167   Hunter Publishing

ABOUT THE AUTHOR

Baye Hunter has been a teacher of adult ESL at the Toronto District School Board since 1988. She has taught all levels. She holds a Bachelor of Education, Bachelor of Arts and a TESL Certificate. She has also taught in Hong Kong and Australia. She co-won with Ann Marie Guy the grand prize at the TESL Ontario Conference for her video "Let's All Go to the AGO" (on youtube.com). Visit her website at www.bayehunter.com for free downloadable activities.

ABOUT THE BOOK

Amazing Theme-Based ESL Worksheets for Beginners is based on vocabulary for the development of language foundations and on the premise that ESL learners must use a word several times in context to be able to remember it. Reading, writing, listening, speaking, grammar and communicative activities are built around the vocabulary. The book has a series of flash cards. These images may be used in various lessons, to introduce and reinforce the vocabulary and language structures.

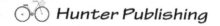 Hunter Publishing

Table of Contents

Community - Vocabulary 1

library	church	airport	barber shop	cafe	fire station
apartment building	mechanic	gym	farm	bank	hospital

1. _____

2. _____

3. _____

4. _____

5. _____

6. _____

7. _____

8. _____

9. _____

10. _____

11. _____

12. _____

Community - Vocabulary 1 Crossword

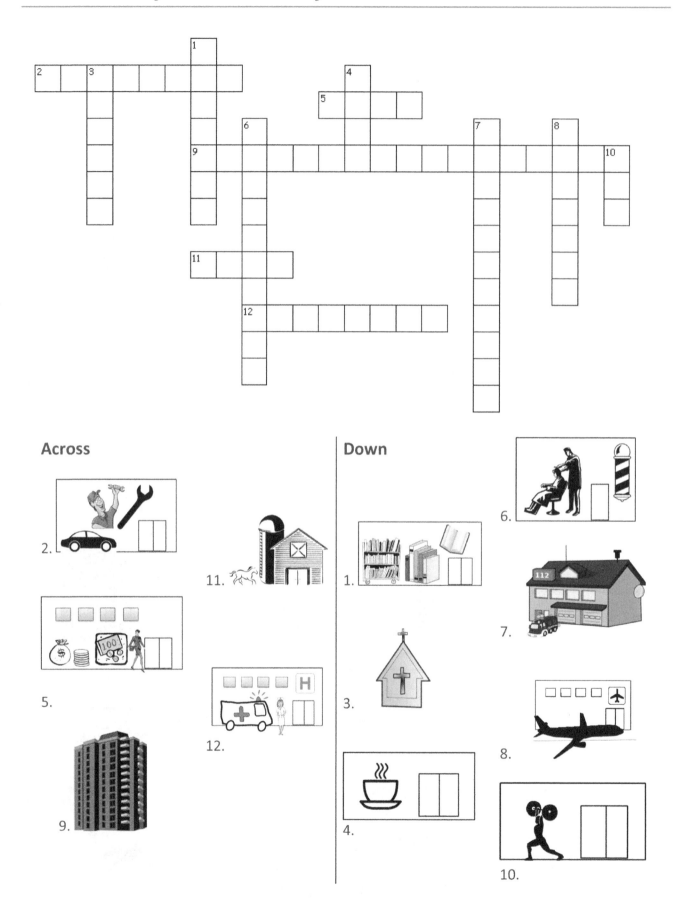

Across

2.

5.

9.

11.

12.

Down

6.

7.

8.

10.

1.

3.

4.

Vocabulary 1 – 'next to'

Where is the library?	It's next to the barber shop.

Make questions about the following with 'next to.'

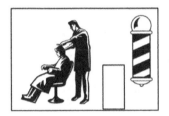

1. Where is the barber shop?   It's next to the library.

2. _____

3. _____

4. _____

 5. _____

 6. _____

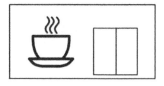 7. _____

 8. _____

 9. _____

 10. _____

 11. _____

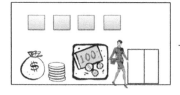 12. _____

Community - Vocabulary 2

| subway station | shopping mall | movie theatre | post office | school | train station |
| park | supermarket | drugstore | hair dresser | mosque | restaurant |

1. _____

2. _____

3. _____

4. _____

5. _____

6. _____

7. _____

8. _____

9. _____

10. _____

11. _____

12. _____

Community - Vocabulary 2 - Crossword

Across

5.

9.

10.

11.

Down

1.

2.

3.

4.

5.

6.

7.

8.

Vocabulary 2 – 'across from'

Where is the restaurant?	It's across from the park.

Make questions about the following with 'across from.'

1. Where is the movie theatre?
   It's across from the post office.

2. _____

3. _____

4. _____

5. _____

6. _____

7. _____

8. _____

9. _____

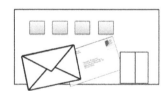

10. _____

11. _____

12. _____

Vocabulary 1 & 2 – Where is John?

Where is Susan?	She is at the bank.
Where is Peter?	He is at the shopping mall.
Where are Susan and Peter?	They are at the gym.
Where are you?	I am at the supermarket.

Make questions and answers about the people in the pictures:

John

1. Where is John?
   He is at the barber shop.

Annette

2. _____

John and Annette

3. _____

Kirti

4. _____

Mary and Paul

5. _____

Sharon

6. _____

Sharon and Kirti

7. _____

you

8. _____

Places in the new community

Last week John moved to a new neighbourhood. The new neighbourhood has many places in the community but it doesn't have others.

Write sentences about the new neighbourhood with 'has' and 'doesn't have.'

Does the neighbourhood have a library? Yes, it has a library.	Does it have a restaurant? No, it doesn't have a restaurant

1. Does it have a barber shop?
   No, it doesn't have a barber shop.

2. _____

3. _____

4. _____

5. _____

6. _____

7. _____

Community - Vocabulary 3

| art gallery | factory | beach | hardware store | bus station | museum |
| office tower | swimming pool | gas station | synagogue | hotel | temple |

1. _____

2. _____

3. _____

4. _____

5. _____

6. _____

7. _____

8. _____

9. _____

10. _____

11. _____

12. _____

Community - Vocabulary 3 - Crossword

Across

1.

8.

10.

11.

5.

12.

Down

2.

4.

6.

7.

9.

Where did they go? - Vocabulary 3

Make questions and answers in the past tense:

 Mary — last Saturday 1. *Where did **Mary** go **last Saturday**?*
*She **went** to the **swimming** pool.*

 John and Kayla — on Friday  2. _____

 Arnold — last night  3. _____

 mom and dad — last week  4. _____

 your sister — on Tuesday morning  5. _____

 Joe's brother — yesterday  6. _____

 uncle Tom — yesterday morning  7. _____

 Mr. Smith and Mr. Cooper — last month 8. _____

Unscramble

Unscramble the following words to find the places in the community:

TRA RYALEGL ☐☐☐ ☐☐☐☐☐☐☐₉

TYRCAOF ☐☐☐☐☐☐☐₁

HEACB ☐☐☐☐☐

REAHRWAD ROSET ☐☐☐☐☐☐☐☐ ☐☐☐☐☐₂

UBS NITSOTA ☐☐☐ ☐☐☐☐☐☐₆

SUEMUM ☐☐☐☐☐☐₃

FIOFEC TOEWR ☐☐☐☐☐☐₇ ☐☐☐☐☐

NIIMWSMG PLOO ☐☐☐☐☐☐☐☐₄ ☐☐☐☐

GSA ITSOANT ☐☐☐ ☐☐☐☐☐☐☐₈

SYGNOEAUG ☐☐☐☐☐☐☐☐☐₅

LEOHT ☐☐☐☐☐

PELETM ☐☐☐☐☐☐

☐☐☐☐☐☐☐☐☐
1 2 3 4 5 6 7 8 9

It's on the corner of

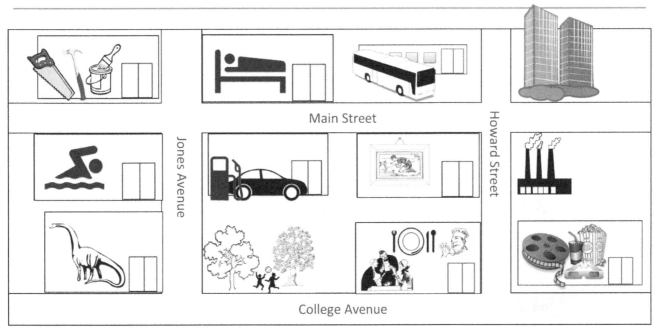

Main Street

Jones Avenue

Howard Street

College Avenue

Make questions about the following with 'on the corner of.'

1. Where is the hardware store?

It's **on the corner of** Main Street and Jones Avenue.

2. _____

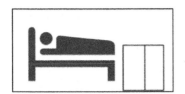

3. _____

4. _____

5. _____

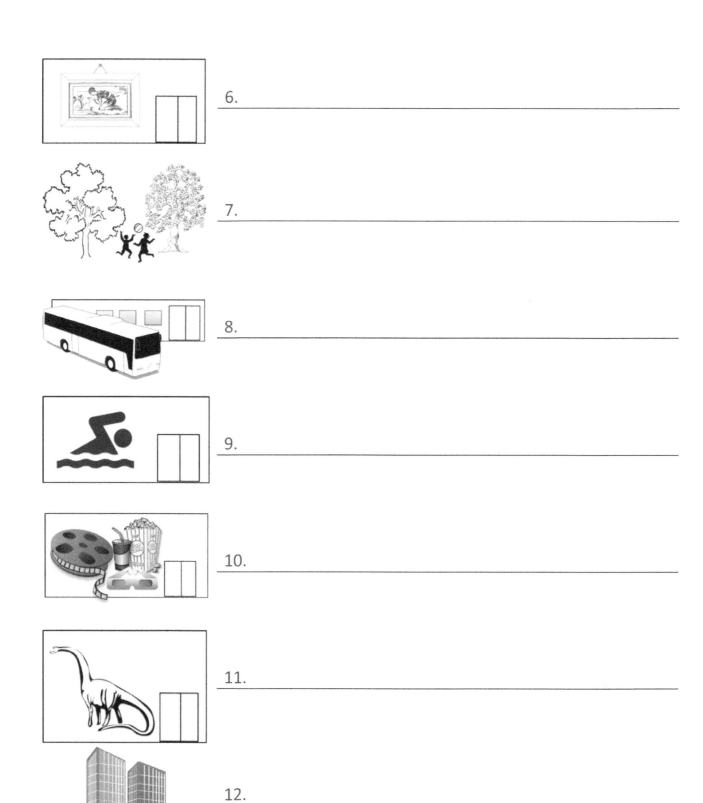

6. _____

7. _____

8. _____

9. _____

10. _____

11. _____

12. _____

Community - Vocabulary 4

port	zoo	courthouse	garbage dump	police station	city hall	stadium
bar	florist	laundromat	book store	stationery store	cemetery	bakery

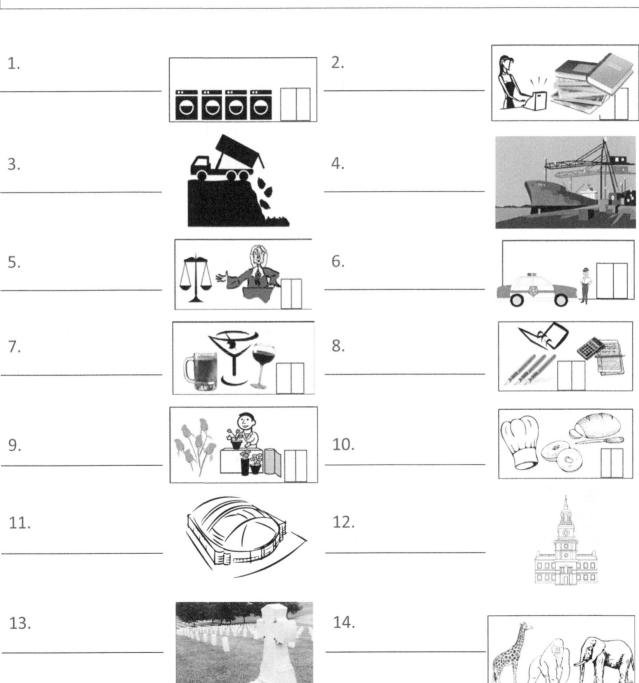

1. _____

2. _____

3. _____

4. _____

5. _____

6. _____

7. _____

8. _____

9. _____

10. _____

11. _____

12. _____

13. _____

14. _____

Community - Vocabulary 4 - Crossword

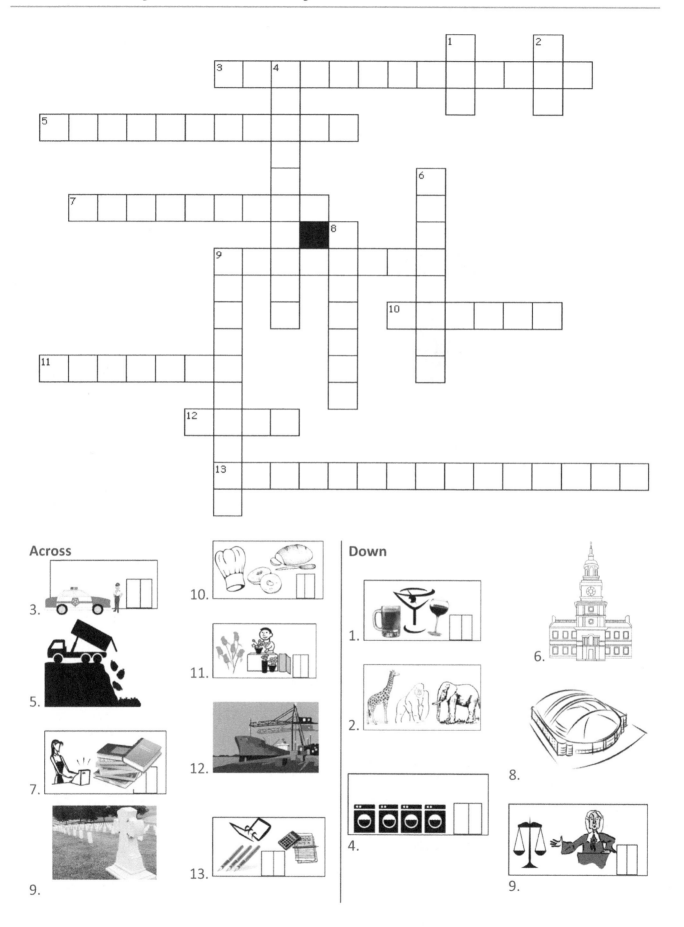

Across

3.

5.

7.

9.

10.

11.

12.

13.

Down

1.

2.

4.

6.

8.

9.

Where are they?

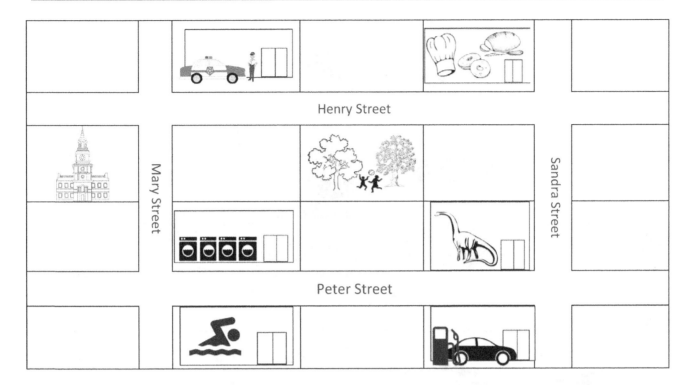

Henry Street

Mary Street

Sandra Street

Peter Street

North

West ← → East

South

Write the names on the map in the correct locations:

1. The stadium is between the police station and the bakery.

2. The barber shop is between the museum and the laundromat.

3. The restaurant is next to the park and across from the city hall.

4. The café is across from the city hall and the police station on the north-west corner.

5. The courthouse is between the swimming pool and the gas station.

6. The zoo is across from the gas station on the south-east corner.

7. The library is next to the park and the museum and across from the bakery.

8. The gym is across from the museum, to the east.

9. The school is next to the city hall and across from the laundromat.

10. The florist is across from the school and across from the swimming pool on the south-west corner.

11. The movie theatre is next to the gym and across from the library.

12. The garbage dump is across from the bakery and across from the movie theatre.

Yes or No?

Stephanie Street

University Avenue

Chalmers Street

Clark Street

Answer the questions with "Yes, it is." or "No, it isn't."

1. Is the swimming pool across from the movie theatre? Yes, it is.
2. Is the garbage dump across from the barber shop?
3. Is the gas station next to the mechanic shop?
4. Is the bakery near the city hall?
5. Is the drugstore across from the supermarket?
6. Is the park next to the swimming pool?
7. Is the temple between the florist and the drugstore?
8. Is the gym across from the school?
9. Is the bar across from the swimming pool?
10. Is the museum next to the hardware store?
11. Is the florist across from the bakery?
12. Is the city hall on Clark Street?
13. Is the garbage dump next to the supermarket.
14. Is the courthouse between the swimming pool and the gym?
15. Is the bar on the corner of Stephanie and Chalmers Street?
16. Is the hardware store across from the school?

Prepositions

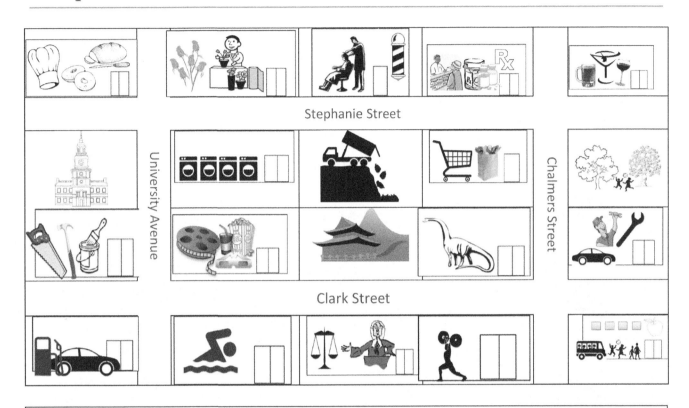

Stephanie Street

University Avenue

Chalmers Street

Clark Street

next to/ beside	between	across from	on the corner of

Put the prepositions in the sentences:

1. The bakery is _____ Stephanie Street and University Avenue.
2. The garbage dump is _____ the laundromat and the supermarket.
3. The museum is _____ the gym.
4. The movie theatre is _____ the temple.
5. The hardware store is _____ the gas station.
6. The courthouse is _____ the swimming pool and the gym.
7. The school is _____ of Clark Street and Chalmers Street.
8. The laundromat is _____ the florist.
9. The barber shop is _____ the florist and the pharmacy.
10. The bakery is _____ the city hall.
11. The bar is _____ Stephanie Street and Chalmers Street.
12. The pharmacy is _____ the supermarket and _____ the barber shop.
13. The mechanic is _____ the park.
14. The temple is _____ the museum and the movie theatre.
15. The swimming pool is _____ the court house.

Review

Match the community place with its name:

   1.   a) restaurant

   2.   b) airport

   3.   c) swimming pool

   4.   d) supermarket

   5.   e) farm

   6.   f) school

   7.   g) hospital

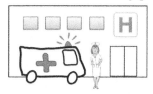   8.   h) bakery

 9. i) art gallery

 10. j) mechanic

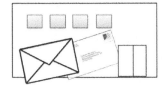 11. k) factory

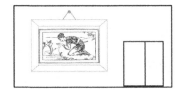 12. l) playground

 13. m) daycare

14. n) train station

 15. o) post office

 16. p) library

A or An?

Put a or an in the following sentences:

1. It's ____a____ port.

2. It's _____ zoo.

3. It's _____ escalator.

4. It's _____ courthouse.

5. It's _____ art gallery.

6. It's _____ garbage dump.

7. It's _____ stadium.

8. It's _____ florist.

9. It's _____ apartment building.

10. It's _____ cemetery.

11. It's _____ underground parking lot.

12. It's _____ factory.

13. It's _____ union office.

14. It's _____ hotel.

15. It's _____ ice rink.

16. It's _____ hairdresser.

17. It's _____ staircase.

18. It's _____ ultrasound clinic.

19. It's _____ entrance.

20. It's _____ office tower.

21. It's _____ airport.

22. It's _____ hardware store.

23. It's _____ x-ray clinic.

24. It's _____ bus station.

25. It's _____ union office.

26. It's _____ museum.

27. It's _____ elevator.

28. It's _____ fire escape.

29. It's _____ expensive store.

30. It's _____ daycare.

31. It's _____ umbrella factory.

32. It's _____ library.

33. It's _____ excellent restaurant.

34. It's _____ university.

35. It's _____ college.

36. It's _____ ugly building.

37. It's _____ beautiful park.

38. It's _____ incinerator.

39. It's _____ stop sign.

Where should you go?

restaurant	library	cemetery	hospital	gym
bank	mechanic	laundromat	dentist office	drugstore
park	shopping mall	post office	school	airport
art gallery	theatre	museum	hardware store	hairdresser

1. You want to send a letter. _____

2. You are very sick or hurt. _____

3. You want to put your money in a safe place. _____

4. You want to see dinosaurs and fossils. _____

5. You want to take a trip. _____

6. You want to learn something new. _____

7. You want to see a play. _____

8. You need to buy a hammer. _____

9. You want to see paintings and sculptures. _____

10. You want to buy some clothes and boots. _____

11. You need to fill a prescription. _____

12. You need your hair cut. _____

13. You would like to have a picnic. _____

14. You are hungry and want something to eat. _____

15. You need some exercise and it's cold outside. _____

16. You want to borrow books, videos or CDs. _____

17. You need to have your teeth cleaned. _____

18. You want to visit a dead family member. _____

19. You need to clean your clothes. _____

20. You have a problem with your car. _____

Can and Can't

Put can or can't (can't = cannot) in the following sentences:

1. You __can__ park .

9. You _____ walk your dog here.

2. You _____ enter.

10. You _____ cross the street here.

3. You _____ go both ways.

11. You _____ drive a car here.

4. You _____ make a U-turn.

12. You _____ make a phone call here.

5. You _____ make a U-turn.

13. You _____ smoke here.

6. You _____ read here.

14. You _____ ride a bicycle here.

7. You _____ make noise here.

15. You _____ turn left. You _____ turn right.

8. You _____ stop here.

16. You _____ recycle here.

Where do they work?

I			He	
you	} work		She	} works
we				
they				

She's a doctor.   1.

He's a pharmacist.   2.

They are teachers.   3.

He's an usher.   4.

She's a lawyer.   5.

I am a fire fighter.   6.

She's a professor.   7.

We are bakers.   8.

He's a salesperson.   9.

We are chefs.   10.

I'm a soccer player.   11.

They are bartenders.   12.

We are factory workers.   13.

He's a priest.   14.

They are lifeguards.   15.

He's a farmer.   16.

She's a driver.   17.

I'm a librarian.   18.

We are fire fighters.   19.

a. _____ in a theatre.

b. _____ in a courthouse.

c. _____ in a drugstore.

d. _____ in a university.

e. _____ in a school.

f. _____ in a store.

g. _She works_ in a hospital.

h. _____ in a fire station.

i. _____ in a stadium.

j. _____ in a bakery.

k. _____ on a farm.

l. _____ in a factory.

m. _____ in a taxi.

n. _____ in a fire station.

o. _____ in a bar.

p. _____ in a restaurant.

q. _____ in a library.

r. _____ in a pool.

s. _____ in a church.

Safe or Dangerous?

short	old	dangerous	bad	short
small	bright	~~near~~	quiet	expensive

Find the word that means the opposite, then make a question and answer with no and a phrase:

opposite

far ___*near*___   1. Is the airport far?

No, it's near.

large _____   2. _____

cheap _____   3. _____

noisy _____   4. _____

tall _____   5. _____

new_____   6. _____

dark_____   7. _____

long_____   8. _____

good_____   9. _____

safe_____   10. _____

library	hotel	zoo	port	hospital
swimming pool	park	office tower	airport	restaurant

29

Comparisons: One syllable adjectives

cheap > cheap**er**	wide > wid**er**	big > big**ger**

Add **–er** or **–r** to one-syllable adjectives

Double the last letter with adjectives that end in consonant-vowel-consonant

Use the comparative to compare 2 things: The café is **cheaper than** the restaurant.

Make sentences comparing the two places or things:

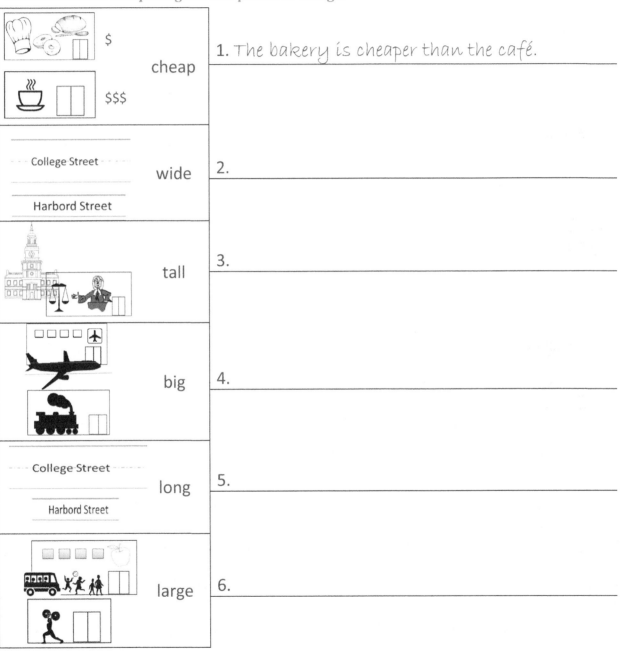

cheap	1. The bakery is cheaper than the café.
wide	2.
tall	3.
big	4.
long	5.
large	6.

cafe	school	airport	gym
train station	courthouse	bakery	city hall

30

Comparisons: Two syllable adjectives ending in -y

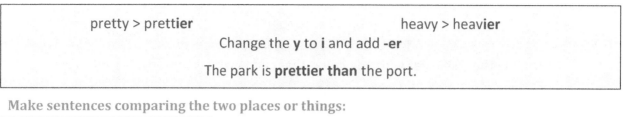

pretty > prett**ier**   heavy > heav**ier**
Change the **y** to **i** and add **-er**
The park is **prettier than** the port.

Make sentences comparing the two places or things:

windy

1. The beach is **windier than** the park.

heavy

2.

messy

3.

noisy

4.

busy

5.

healthy

6.

| beach | gym | park | car | bicycle | garbage dump |
| cemetery | cafe | airport | book store | supermarket | train station |

Comparisons: Two or more syllable adjectives

beautiful > more beautiful	expensive > more expensive
The park is **more beautiful than** the beach.	

Make sentences comparing the two places or things:

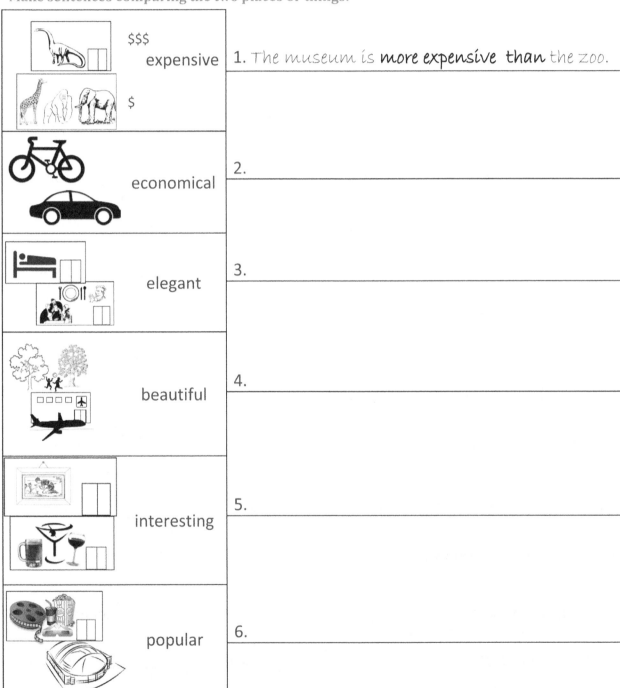

$$$ expensive $	1. The museum is **more expensive than** the zoo.
economical	2.
elegant	3.
beautiful	4.
interesting	5.
popular	6.

bicycle	hotel	zoo	museum	car	stadium
art gallery	airport	bar	movie theatre	park	restaurant

For Sale

House	Apartment
60 years old	5 years old
$700,000	$500,000
2000 square feet	800 square feet
2km from work	10km from work
taxes $2000/year	taxes $1000/year
quiet neighbourhood	noisy neighbourhood

Fill in the blanks with the comparative form:

Sally wants to buy a house or an apartment. She is looking at 2 places. She can't

decide. The house is _____ than the apartment. It's _____ but
                1. old   2. clean

_____. The house is _____ to work, but it is
  3. expensive   4. close

_____ from a supermarket. The apartment is _____ and
  5. far   6. small

_____ to clean. The taxes are _____ but the neighbourhood is
  7. easy   8. low

_____. The apartment has a _____ park near by.
  9. noisy   10. beautiful

The house is _____ and the apartment is _____.
            11. elegant   12. modern

The neighbours are _____. The subway station is _____ and
              13. friendly   14. close

the gym is _____. The street parking is _____ and the
          15. convenient   16. good

recreational opportunities are _____.
                       17. accessible

The apartment is also _____ and has _____ ceilings. The
              18. bright   19. high

kitchen and bathroom are _____ and in _____ condition.
                20. dirty   21. worse

The kitchen is _____ but the bathroom is _____.
         22. big   23. tiny

Superlative Places

long	famous	tall	large

1. The Great Wall of China is _____the longest_____ wall in the world.
2. The CN Tower is _____ tower in Canada.
3. Russia is _____ country in the world.
4. The Eiffel Tower is _____ tower in Europe.

cold	slow	fast	good

5. China has _____ train in the world.
6. Cambodia has _____ train in the world.
7. Seychelles has_____beaches in the world.
8. Yellowknife is _____city in Canada.

deep	famous	old	big

9. France has _____ art galleries in the world.
10. The Smithsonian Institute is _____ museum complex in the world.
11. Athens is _____ city in Europe.
12. The Pacific Ocean is _____ ocean in the world.

healthy	small	populated	long

13. Vatican City is _____ country in the world.
14. Iceland has _____ people in the world.
15. Japan has _____ living people in the world.
16. China is _____ country in the world.

polluted	high	salty	hot

17. Dallol, Ethiopia in Africa is_____ place in the world.
18. Ahwaz, Iran is_____ town in the world.
19. Angel Falls, Venezuela is _____ waterfall in the world.
20. Don Juan Pond – Antarctica is _____ place in the world.

Answering questions

1. What street is your school on?_____

2. What street do you live on?_____

3. What number do you live at?_____

4. What street does your partner next to you live on?_____

5. Are there any libraries in your neighbourhood?_____

6. What is the name of the library nearest you?_____

7. What street is there nearest fire station on?_____

8. What is the closest shopping mall?_____

9. Do you live in a house or an apartment?_____

10. Do you prefer a house or an apartment?_____

11. Do you like to go to cafes?_____

12. Are there many cats and dogs in your neighbourhood?_____

13. Where is the closest bank to your house?_____

14. How long does it take you to get to school?_____

15. How do you get to school?_____

16. Where is your doctor's office?_____

17. Where do you buy groceries?_____

18. What is the nearest subway station to your house?_____

19. Do you have parking at your home?_____

20. Where is the closest streetcar or bus to your home?_____

21. Where is the nearest park to your home?_____

22. How far is the park?_____

23. Where is the closest hardware store?_____

24. Where is the closest swimming pool?_____

Is there a bakery in the neighbourhood?

> **Is there** <u>a bakery</u> in the neighbourhood?
> **Are there any** <u>swimming pools</u> in the neighbourhood?

Put 'Is there' and 'Are there any' in the following sentences:

1. _____ movie theatres in the neighbourhood?

2. _____ a dance studio in the neighbourhood?

3. _____ a factory in the neighbourhood?

4. _____ cafes in the neighbourhood?

5. _____ a church in the neighbourhood?

6. _____ fire stations in the neighbourhood?

7. _____ shopping malls in the neighbourhood?

8. _____ a mosque in the neighbourhood?

9. _____ libraries in the city?

10. _____ variety stores in the community?

11. _____ an office tower in the community?

12. _____ a subway station in the neighbourhood?

13. _____ ice cream parlours in the neighbourhood?

14. _____ a stadium in the city?

15. _____ a police station in the neighbourhood?

16. _____ bars in the neighbourhood?

17. _____ barber shops in the neighbourhood?

18. _____ a hospital in the neighbourhood?

19. _____ a swimming pool in the neighbourhood?

20. _____ art galleries in the neighbourhood?

How many are there?

how many	how far	where	are there any

Put the question words in for each question:

1. __How many__ hospitals are there in Newtown? There are 10 hospitals in Newtown.

2. _____ is the laundromat? It's across from the museum.

3. _____ banks on Yonge Street? Yes, there are many.

4. _____ is the museum? It's near John and Charles Streets.

5. _____ is the mechanic from Atwell Street? It's 3 blocks.

6. _____ airports in Richton? No, there aren't.

7. _____ is the airport from downtown? It's 20 kilometres.

8. _____ is the supermarket? It's between the church and the stadium.

9. _____ is the factory from here? It's 6 blocks.

10. _____ is the bar? It's around the corner from the bakery.

Is there or Are there?

Make questions about the following pictures:

1. Is there a movie theatre in the neighbourhood?

2. Are there any apartment buildings in the neighnourhood?

3. _____

4. _____

5. _____

37

Where are they going?

1. John is going to the factory.

2. Sharon and Susie

3. Albert and I

4. I

5. Peter and Hank

beach	subway station	hardware store	factory	zoo

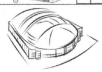

6. She

7. Stephanos, Nick and Sue

8. We

9. Antoine and I

10. You

pharmacy	stadium	restaurant	library	park

Where do they work?

I
You
We
They
} work

He
She
It
} works

He's a fork lift operator.

1. He works in a factory.

She's a baker.

2. _____

_____

He's an accountant.

3. _____

_____

They are nurses.

4. _____

_____

| bakery | ~~factory~~ | hospital | office tower |

They are chefs.

5. _____

_____

He's a mechanic.

6. _____

_____

He's a pilot.

7. _____

_____

He's a soccer player.

8. _____

_____

| stadium | airport | restaurant | garage |

They are pharmacists.

9. _____

_____

She's a farmer.

10. _____

_____

I am a teacher.

11. _____

_____

He's an eye doctor.

12. _____

_____

| clinic | school | drugstore | farm |

She's a police officer.

They are assembly workers.

She's a waitress.

We are musicians.

13. _____

14. _____

15. _____

16. _____

_____

_____

_____

_____

| restaurant | police station | concert hall | factory |

She's a hairdresser.

She's a secretary.

He's an usher.

He's a tennis player.

17. _____

18. _____

19. _____

20. _____

_____

_____

_____

_____

| office tower | movie theatre | stadium | hair salon |

She's a daycare worker.

She's a cleaner.

He's a dishwasher.

He's an artist.

21. _____

22. _____

23. _____

24. _____

_____

_____

_____

_____

| hotel | restaurant | studio | daycare |

 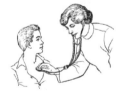

He's a butcher.

I'm a waiter.

She's a doctor.

He's an engineer.

25. _____

26. _____

27. _____

28. _____

_____

_____

_____

_____

| hospital | supermarket | construction site | restaurant |

Where do they live?

I work **in** a shopping mall. a bank. a daycare	She works **on** College Street. They work **at** 215 Huron Street.	We live **in** Montreal. They eat **in** a restaurant. He lives **in** France.

Put *in*, *on* or *at* in the following sentences:

1. I work _____ a school.
   I work _____ 77 York Street.
   I work_____ New York.

2. He lives _____ Mable Street.
   He works _____ a fire hall.
   He lives _____ Halifax.

3. They eat _____Church Street.
   They eat_____ a bar.
   They work_____ 99 Front St.

4. We live _____ Canada.
   We live _____ an apartment.
   We live _____ Bloor Street.

5. She works _____a bank.
   She works _____89 John Ave.
   She works _____Vancouver.

6. You eat _____ a hotel.
   You eat _____ Peter Street.
   You eat _____ Toronto.

7. You work _____ an office.
   You work _____ Cal Street.
   You work_____ 19 Shule Rd.

8. He lives _____ Regina.
   He works _____ a university.
   He lives _____ 19 Main St.

9. We eat _____a mall.
   We eat_____ Market Street.
   We work_____ 72 Charles St.

10. We live _____ a house.
    We live _____ 91 Court Rd.
    We live _____ Ohio.

11. She works _____a church.
    She works _____St Clair Ave.
    She works _____Toronto.

12. You eat _____ 29 Mark St.
    You eat _____ bakery.
    You eat _____ Chicago.

Adverbs of Frequency/Simple Present

Modes of transportation

always	We use these adverbs of frequency with
usually	the simple present tense.
often	
sometimes	I always walk to school.
seldom	He sometimes rides his bike.
rarely	We rarely drive the car.
never	They never take a taxi.

Make sentences about the following using the adverbs of frequency. Make the question with "How often..." and answer the question about yourself:

1. take the bus > *How often do you take the bus? I rarely take the bus.*

2. take a taxi_____

3. ride a bicycle_____

4. drive a car_____

5. drive a truck_____

6. fly in a plane_____

7. take a streetcar_____

8. take the subway_____

9. walk_____

10. ride a motorcycle_____

11. ride in a car_____

12. go hiking_____

13. go for a walk_____

14. ride in a helicopter_____

15. hitch hike_____

It's at 25 Charles Street

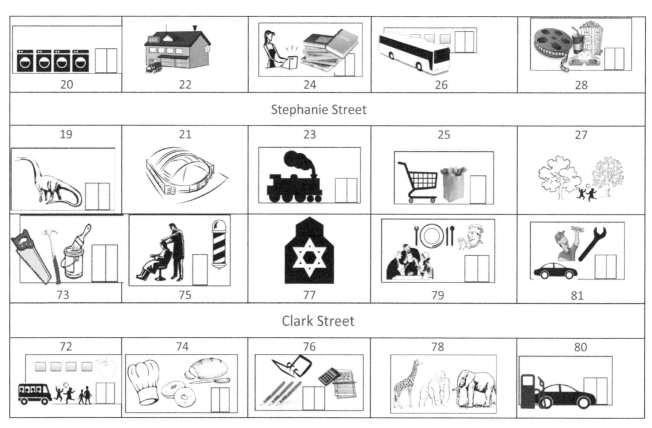

20	22	24	26	28

Stephanie Street

19	21	23	25	27

73	75	77	79	81

Clark Street

72	74	76	78	80

Write questions and answers about the following:

1. Where is the fire hall?

It's at 22 Stephanie Street. It's on Stephanie Street.

2. _____

3. _____

4. _____

5. _____

stationery store	fire hall	synagogue	stadium	museum

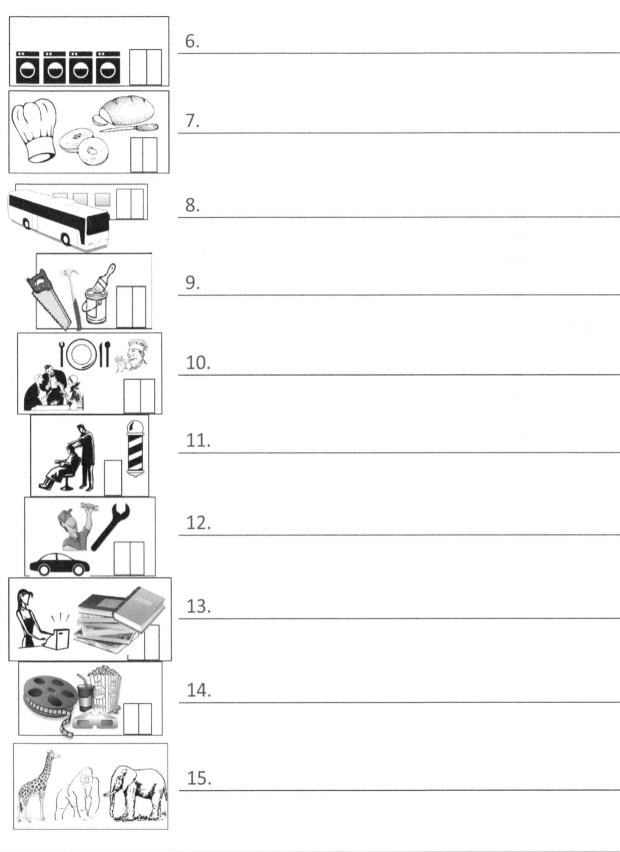

6. _____

7. _____

8. _____

9. _____

10. _____

11. _____

12. _____

13. _____

14. _____

15. _____

| mechanic | zoo | movie theatre | barber shop | book store |
| hardware store | laundromat | restaurant | bus station | bakery |

How do I get from the farm to the zoo?

walk up walk down	on the right on the left	across from next to

City Street

 Excuse me. How do I get from the bank to the beach?

Walk down City Street. The beach is on the right, across from the farm.

Excuse me. How do I get from the farm to the bar?

Walk up City Street. The bar is on the left across from the movie theatre.

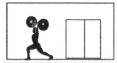

1. Excuse me. How do I get from the beach to the art gallery?

_____

2.

_____

_____

3.

_____

_____

art gallery	beach	bakery
hairdresser	movie theatre	gym

45

4. _____

5. _____

6. _____

7. _____

8. _____

9. _____

10. _____

| bakery | shopping mall | mosque | farm | gym |
| beach | art gallery | garbage dump | bank | |

Listening

Circle the place that the teacher calls out from each row:

	A	B	C	D
1.				
2.				
3.				
4.				
5.				
6.				
7.				
8.				
9.				
10.				

11.

12.

13.

14.

15.

16.

17.

18.

19.

20.

21.

22.

An Accident

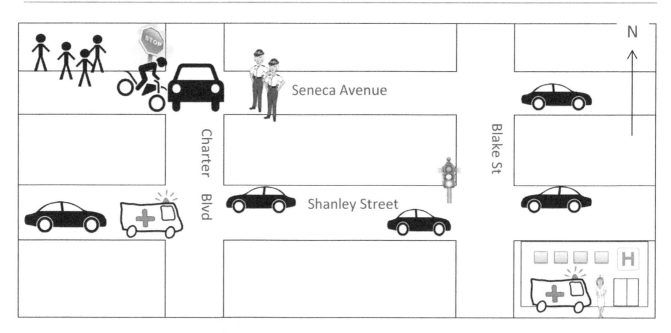

Answer with yes, no or not enough information. Circle the answer.

1.	The accident happened at the corner of Blake and Shanley Street.	yes	no	?
2.	An ambulance is near.	yes	no	?
3.	The hospital is very far away.	yes	no	?
4.	The car didn't stop at the stop sign.	yes	no	?
5.	Shanley Street is one way.	yes	no	?
6.	There are three police offers at the scene.	yes	no	?
7.	The bicycle caused the accident.	yes	no	?
8.	The hospital is full.	yes	no	?
9.	The bicycle was going east on Seneca Ave.	yes	no	?
10.	The car was going south on Charter Boulevard.	yes	no	?
11.	The accident happened at 9:30am.	yes	no	?
12.	Four people saw the accident.	yes	no	?
13.	The bicycle was in the bike lane.	yes	no	?
14.	There is a traffic light at Blake and Shanley.	yes	no	?
15.	The car driver called an ambulance for the cyclist.	yes	no	?
16.	The hospital is on the south-east corner of Blake and Shanley.	yes	no	?
17.	The car driver will be in hospital for a long time.	yes	no	?
18.	There is a nurse and an ambulance waiting outside the hospital.	yes	no	?

In the neighbourhood 1

van	ferry	traffic light	bridge	street lamp
bicycle lane	motorcycle	phone booth	house	helmet
wheelchair accessible	sidewalk	two way street	stop sign	fire hydrant

Match the words with the pictures:

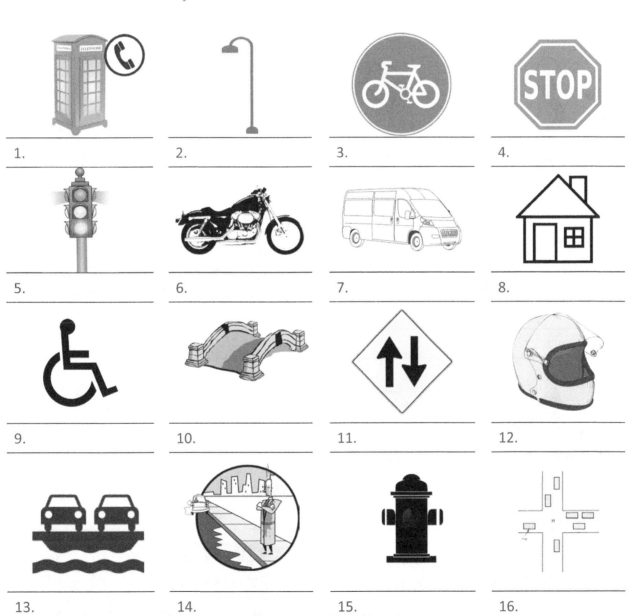

1.

2.

3.

4.

5.

6.

7.

8.

9.

10.

11.

12.

13.

14.

15.

16.

In the neighbourhood 2

garbage can	bus shelter	hiking path	fire escape
highway	pickup truck	garbage truck	accident
elevator	city name sign	transport truck	fire engine
curvy road	bus stop	ambulance	crosswalk

Match the words with the pictures

17.

18.

19.

20.

21.

22.

23.

24.

25.

26.

27.

28.

29.

30.

31.

32.

Actions in the community - 1

eat	watch	walk	shop
pray	drink	swim	read
turn	fix	order	shop
sleep	assemble	wash	run

Match the verbs with the picture

1. _____

2. _____

3. _____

4. _____

5. _____

6. _____

7. _____

8. _____

9. _____

10. _____

11. _____

12. _____

 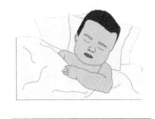  

13. _____

14. _____

15. _____

16. _____

Actions in the community – 1 Crossword

Down

1.

4.

6.

9.

11.

13.

14.

Across

2.

3.

5.

6.

7.

8.

10.

12.

Actions in the community - 2

study	listen	paint	cut
work	ride	play	exercise
stop	wear	talk	cross
hike	bake	fly	drive

17.

18.

19.

20.

21.

22.

23.

24.

25.

26.

27.

28.

29.

30.

31.

32.

Actions in the community – 2 - Crossword

Across

3.

4.

6.

9.

10.

11.

13.

14.

Down

1.

2.

5.

6.

7.

8.

9.

12.

Where do these things happen?

Match the verb with the place that these things are done. Find the best answer:

study	a)	1.	bakery	
work	b)	2.	art studio	
stop	c)	3.	phone booth	
hike	d)	4.	bike lane	
listen	e)	5.	office tower	
ride	f)	6.	library	
bake	g)	7.	intersection	
paint	h)	8.	hiking trail	
play	i)	9.	crosswalk	
talk	j)	10.	airport	
fly	k)	11.	concert hall	
cut	l)	12.	playground	
exercise	m)	13.	church	
cross	n)	14.	gym	
drive	o)	15.	barber shop	
fix	p)	16.	mechanic	
pray	q)	17.	highway	

-ING Endings

Add –ing to most words	Take off the final e in words ending in –e	Do not double
	bak~~e~~ > baking	w, x, y
If the word ends in Consonant-Vowel-Consonant with the stress on the last syllable, double the last letter		
	shop > shopping órder > ordering	
	CVC	

Add –ing to the following verbs:

1. eat _____
2. stop _____
3. watch _____
4. wear _____
5. walk _____
6. talk _____
7. study _____
8. cross _____
9. talk _____
10. hike _____
11. run _____
12. take _____
13. go _____
14. drive _____
15. shop _____
16. paint _____
17. take _____
18. play _____
19. cook _____
20. ride _____
21. swim _____
22. arrive _____
23. read _____
24. wait _____
25. pray _____
26. exercise _____
27. relax _____
28. leave _____
29. fix _____
30. sing _____
31. drink _____
32. come _____
33. shop _____
34. look _____
35. sleep _____
36. jump _____
37. assemble _____
38. think _____
39. wash _____
40. rain _____
41. listen _____
42. read _____
43. buy _____
44. fix _____
45. cut _____
46. order _____

What are they doing?

Present Continuous

I am eating	It is raining
You are talking	They are sitting
She is studying	We are watching
He is walking	

cook + ing = cooking	take + ing = taking	play + ing = playing	swim + ing = swimming

Use the present continuous in the following sentences:

eat	watch	~~walk~~	study

1. She _____is walking_____ in the park.
2. He _____ at school.
3. We _____ at a restaurant.
4. They _____ a movie at the movie theatre.

pray	drink	swim	read

5. I _____ coffee at a café.
6. He _____ at the church.
7. You _____ at the swimming pool.
8. The children_____ at the library.

relax	fix	drink	shop

9. We _____ at the bar.
10. He_____ at the beach.
11. They_____ at the supermarket.
12. She_____ her car at the mechanic.

sleep	assemble	wash	run

13. He_____ clothes at the laundromat.
14. She_____ at the hotel.
15. They _____ toys at the factory.
16. He_____ at the stadium.

watch	listen	buy	cut

17. They _____ clothes at the shopping mall.
18. They _____ a soccer game at the stadium.
19. She_____ to music at the concert hall.
20. He _____ his hair at the barber shop.

work	ride	play	exercise

21. I _____ at the gym.
22. Tom _____ at the office tower.
23. Sally _____ her bicycle in the bike lane.
24. The children _____ in the playground.

stop	wear	talk	cross

25. I _____ on the phone in the phone booth.
26. John _____ at the intersection.
27. We _____ over the bridge.
28. Carl_____ his helmet.

hike	walk	take	drive

29. We _____ on the sidewalk.
30. I _____ out the garbage to the sidewalk.
31. Sarah_____ the van on the highway.
32. Charles_____ in the park.

play	listen	ride	paint

33. Anne _____ a motorcycle.
34. The artist_____ in the studio.
35. The children _____ to stories in the daycare.
36. The musicians _____ their instruments in the concert hall.

Where are they going?

These are the question words:

who	what	when	where	why	how
They are going to the bank. Where are they going?			She is visiting her grandmother. Who is she visiting?		

Use them in the following sentences:

1. She is going to work. (where)_____ *Where is she going?* _____

2. She is travelling by bus. (how)_____ *How is she travelling?* _____

3. She is arriving at 6pm. (when)_____

4. They are looking at the office tower. (what)_____

5. We are waiting because the bus is late. (why)_____

6. She is visiting her mother. (who)_____

7. You are walking to the park. (where)_____

8. They are driving on the highway (where)_____

9. We are exercising at the gym. (where)_____

10. The bus is leaving at 2:30am. (when)_____

11. She is listening to music. (what)_____

12. Sally and Tom are washing clothes at the laundromat. (where)_____

_____

13. We are singing because it's his birthday.(why)_____

14. She is playing soccer at the stadium. (what)_____

15. She is coming by foot. (how)_____

16. She is looking for Jean. (who)_____

Are they going? No, they aren't going.

Question forms:

Am I shopping?	Is it raining?
Are you walking?	Are we relaxing?
Is he jumping?	Are they playing?
Is she thinking>	

Negative form, long answer:

I am not eating > I'm not eating	It is not raining > It isn't raining
You are not going > You aren't going	We are not driving > We aren't driving
He is not shopping > He isn't shopping	They are not swimming > They aren't swimming
She is not talking > She isn't talking	

Make questions and negative answers:

 1. Is he fixing the car? No, he isn't fixing the car.

 2. _____

 3. _____

 4. _____

read	fix	relax	drink

5. _____

6. _____

7. _____

8. _____

shop	pray	order	run

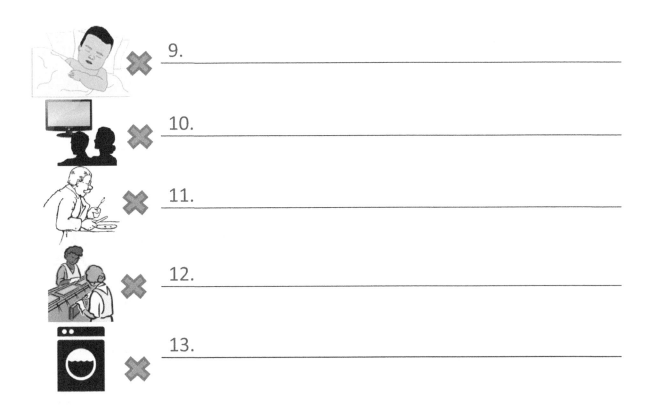

9. _____

10. _____

11. _____

12. _____

13. _____

| eat | sleep | watch | assemble toys | wash |

14. _____

15. _____

16. _____

17. _____

18. _____

| ride | listen | bake | exercise | fly |

Community Verbs – Regular Simple Past Tense

Regular verbs: add –d or –ed | play > played   study > studied

Example: She sharpened the pencil.

What did they do? Make sentences in the past tense:

1.   She exercised.

2.   _____   to music

3.   _____   a cake

4.   _____   his clothes

5.   _____   toys

6.   _____

7.   _____

8.   _____

bake	assemble	relax	listen
exercise	paint	hike	wash

63

9. _____

10. _____

11. _____

12. _____

13. _____

14. _____ a movie

15. _____ with toys

16. _____

watch	study	cross	fix
order	pray	play	shop

Simple Past – Irregular - What did they do?

Make sentences about the following pictures with the verbs below in the past tense:

 some lunch

1. He ate some lunch.

2.

3.

4.

 hair

5.

6.

7.

8.

| run - ran | cut - cut | sleep - slept | drink – drank |
| read - read | eat - ate | drive - drove | fly - flew |

9. _____

10. _____

11. _____

12. _____

 gloves

13. _____

 $$

14. _____

15. *They* _____

16. _____

| go to – went to | wear - wore | read - read | buy - bought |
| swim - swam | drink - drank | take - took | ride - rode |

Scrambled Sentences

Your teacher will dictate 10 sentences to you. Write the phrases in the correct word order:

1. and / between / is / bakery. / hotel / The / bank / the / the

_____

2. and / John / school. / Carlos / to / their / rode / Marie / bikes

_____

3. cafe / for / coffee / to / at / 2 / We / a / a / went / o'clock.

_____

4. is / restaurant / for / The / every / open / 7am / day. / breakfast / at

_____

5. at / for / the / last / park / walk / midnight. / night / a / We / went / in

_____

6. is / on / next / Stratford / zoo / to / downtown. / Avenue / the / mechanic / The

_____

7. the / booth. / are / the / phone / phone / talking / in / You / on

_____

8. at / the / clothes / mall. / They / are / shopping / buying

_____

9. the / sign. / stop / stop / at / didn't / The / car

_____

10. I / get / How / do / the / hospital / office? / the / me. / Excuse / to / from / post

1. The bank is between the hotel and the bakery.

2. John Carlos and Marie rode their bikes to school.

3. We went to a cafe for a coffee at 2 o'clock.

4. The restaurant is open at 7am for breakfast every day.

5. We went for a walk in the park last night at midnight.

6. The mechanic is next to the zoo on Stratford Avenue downtown.

7. You are talking on the phone in the phone booth.

8. They are buying clothes at the shopping mall.

9. The car didn't stop at the stop sign.

10. Excuse me. How do I get from the hospital to the post office?

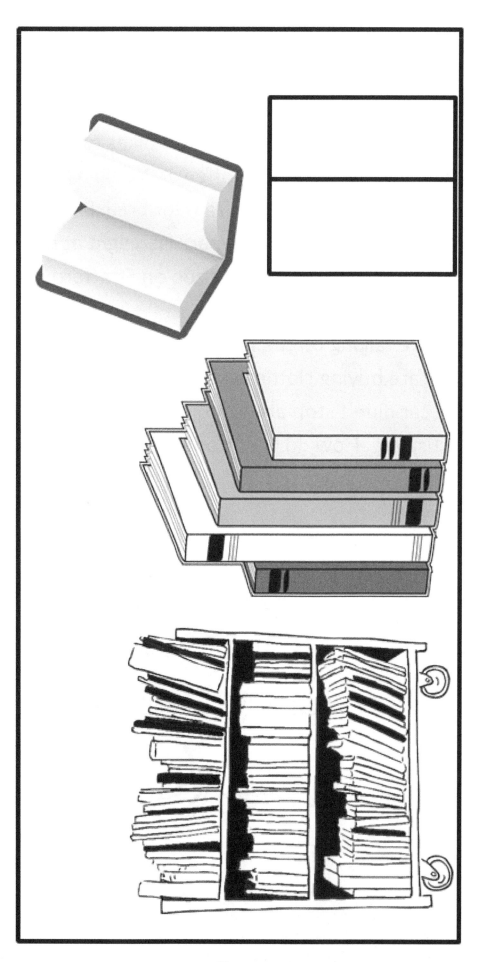

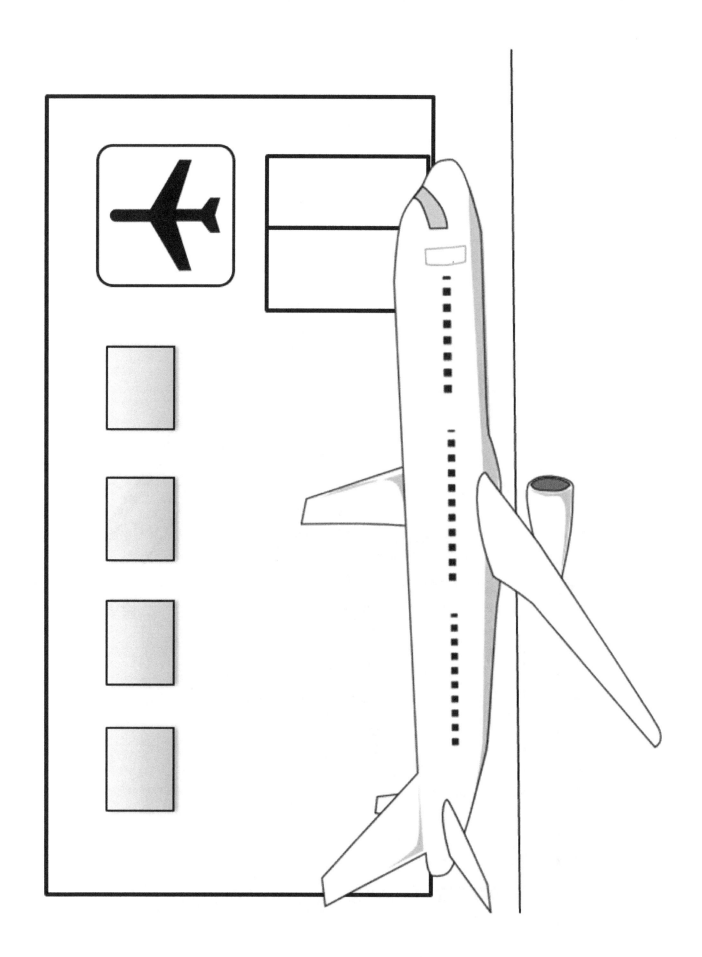

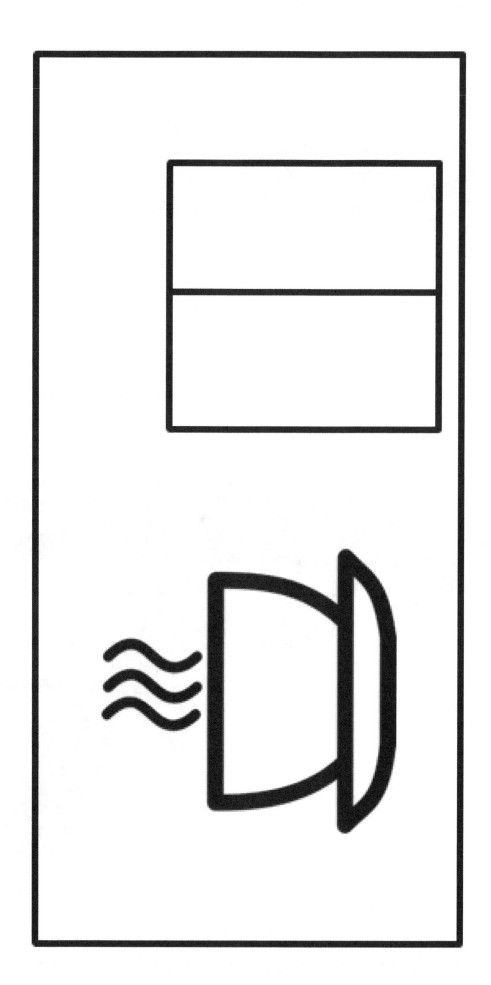

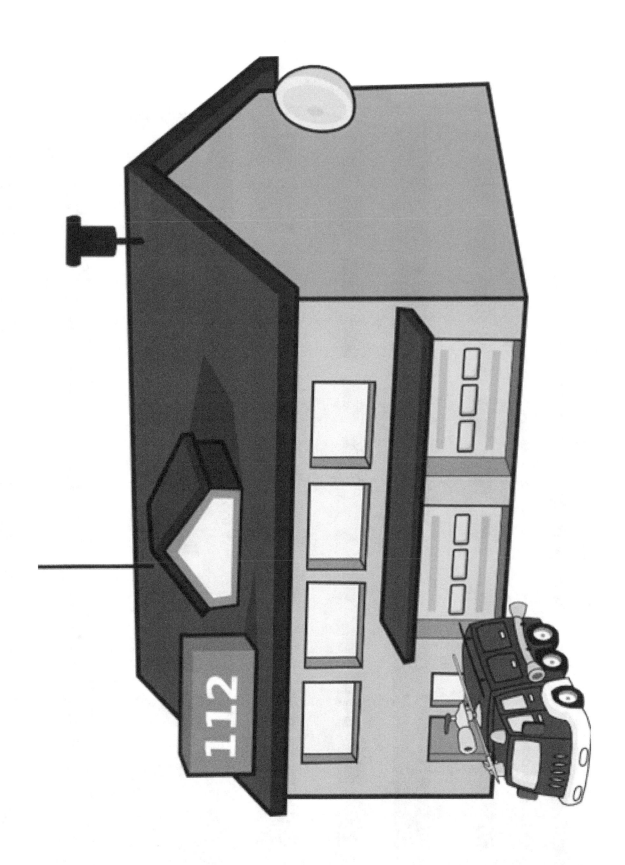

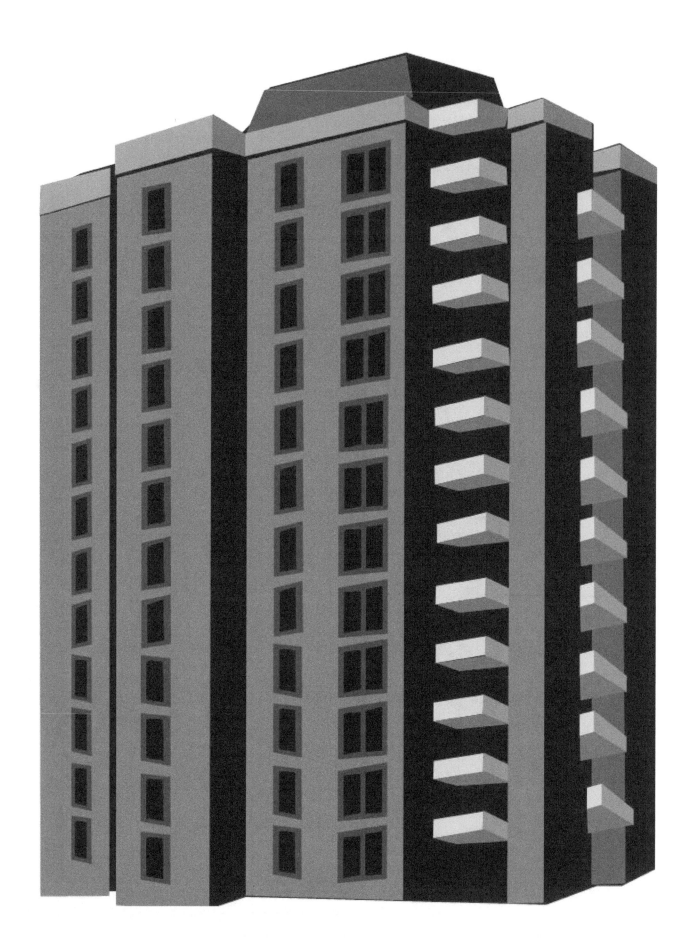

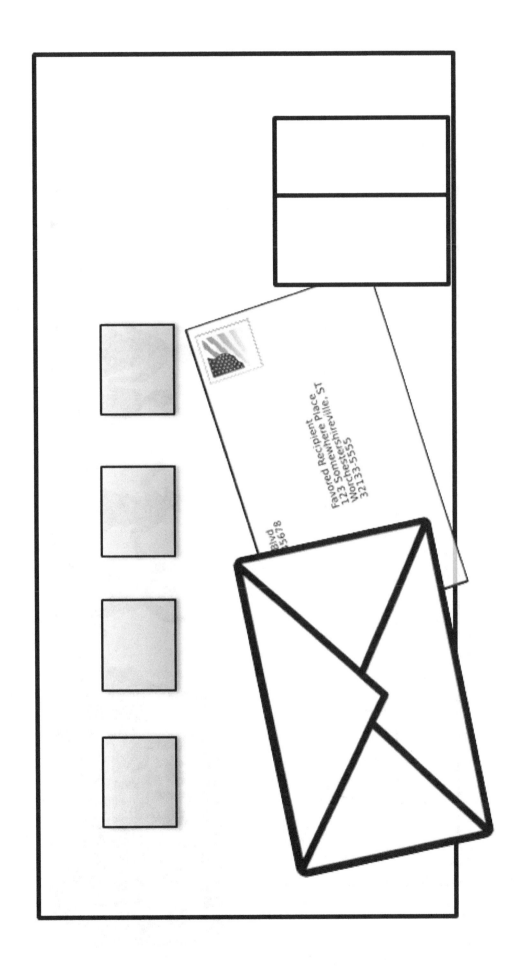

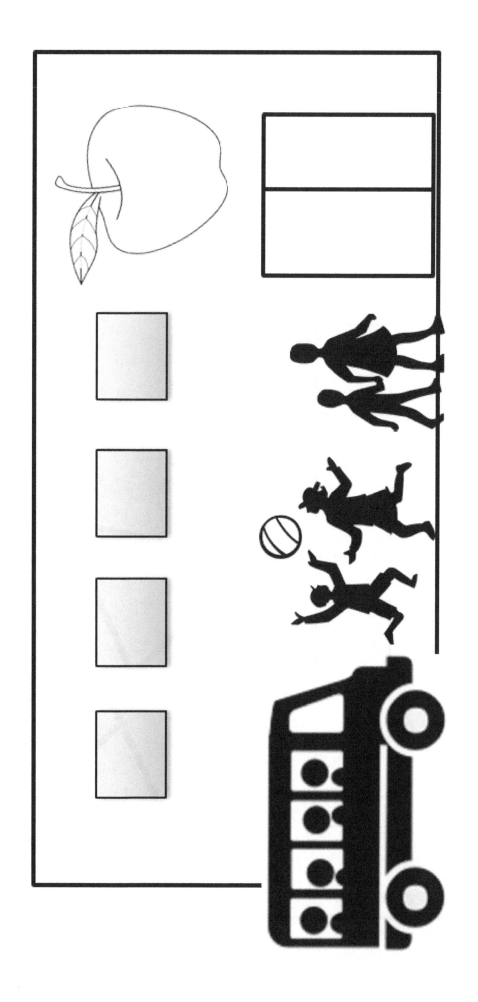

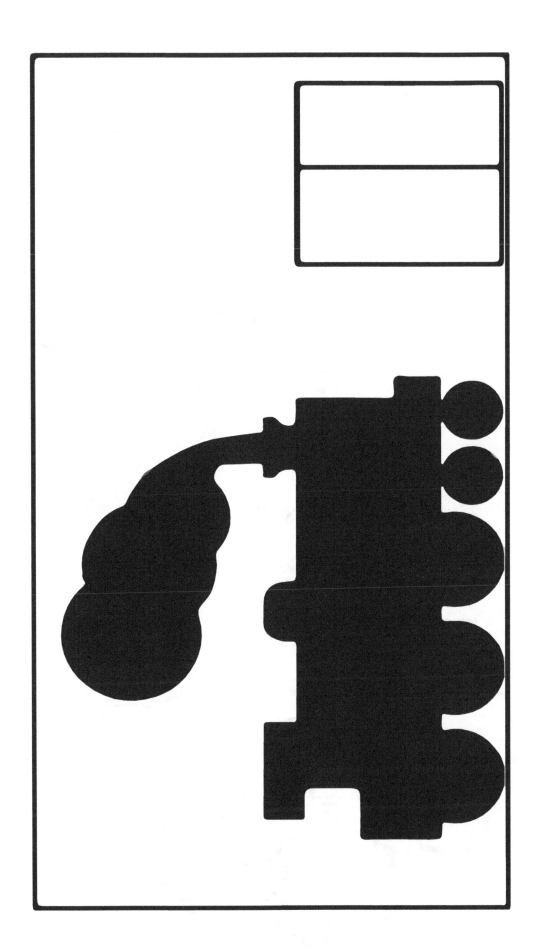

86

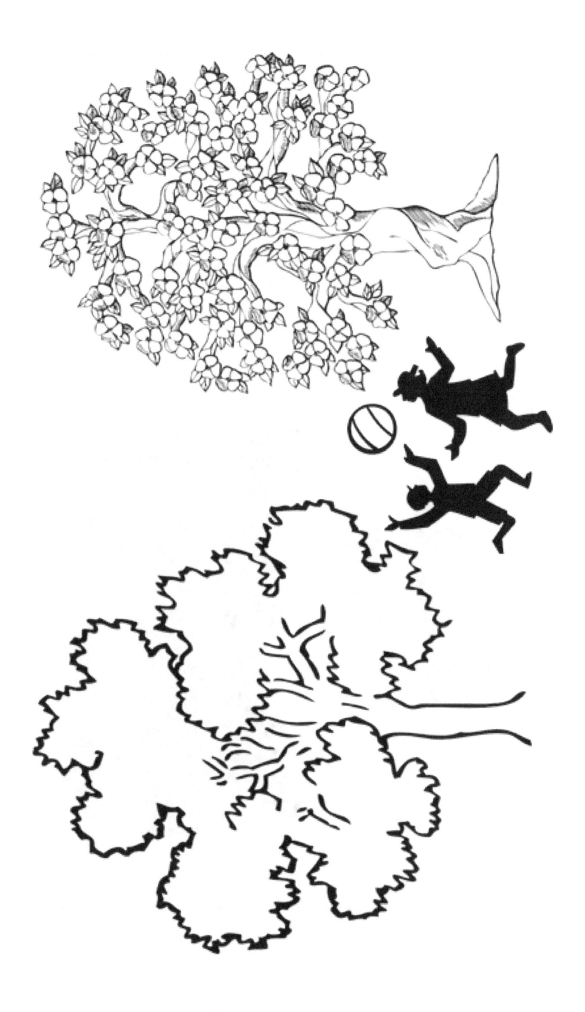

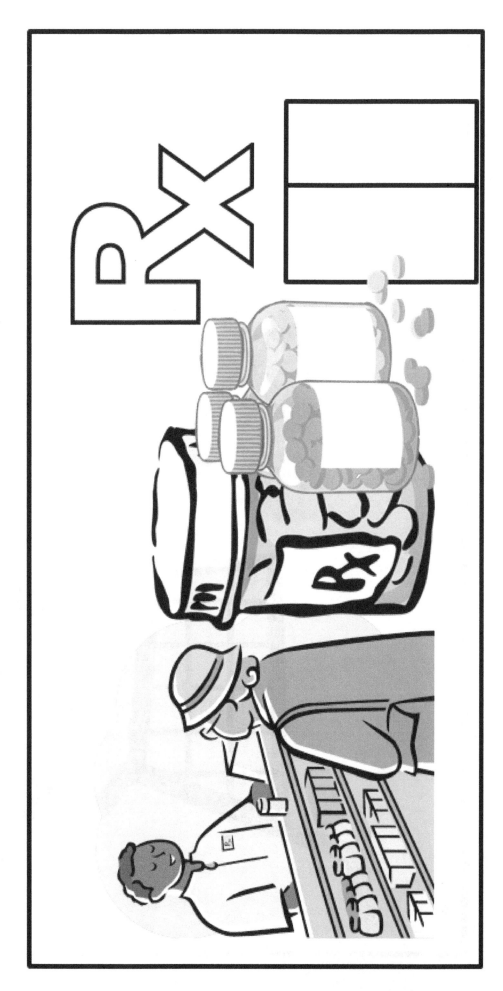

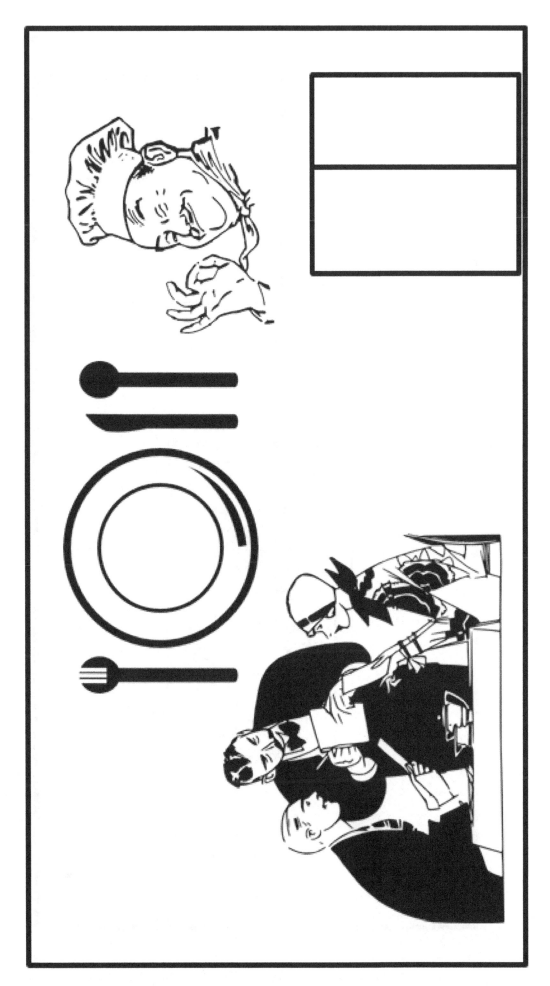

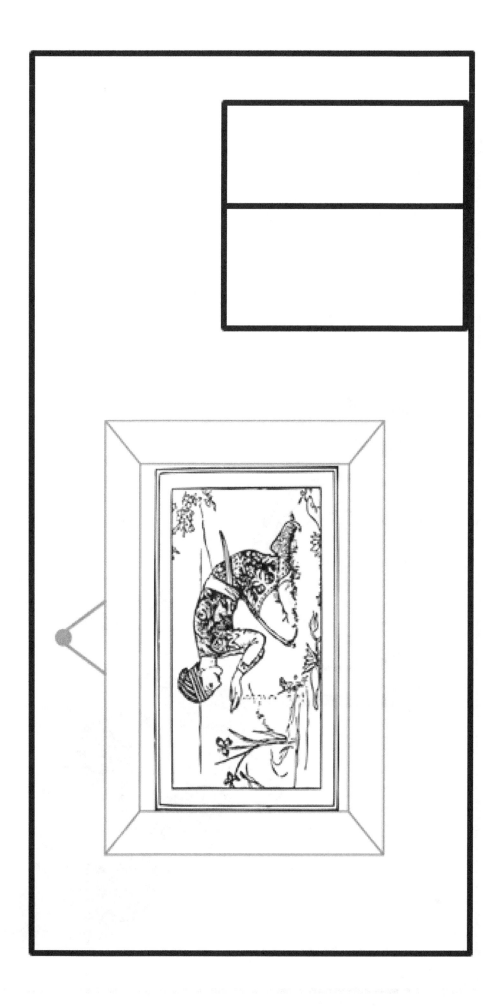

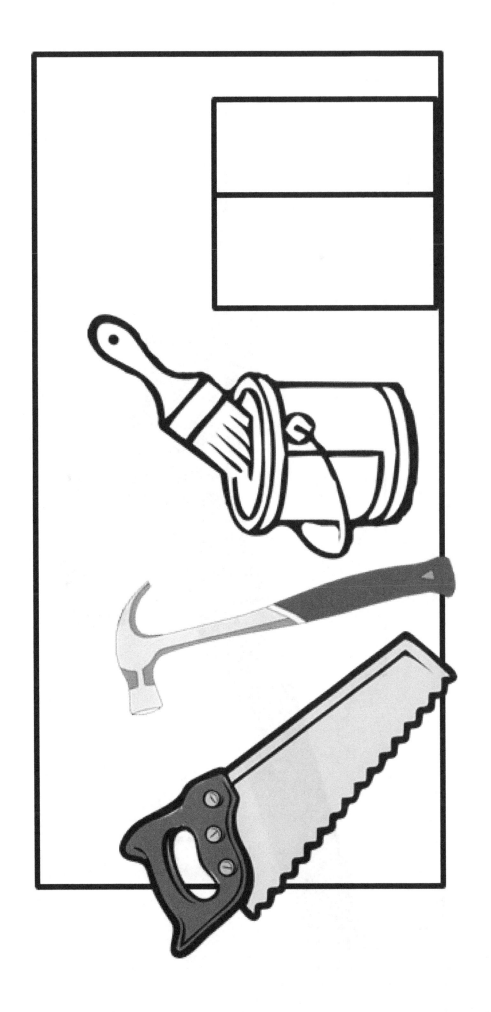

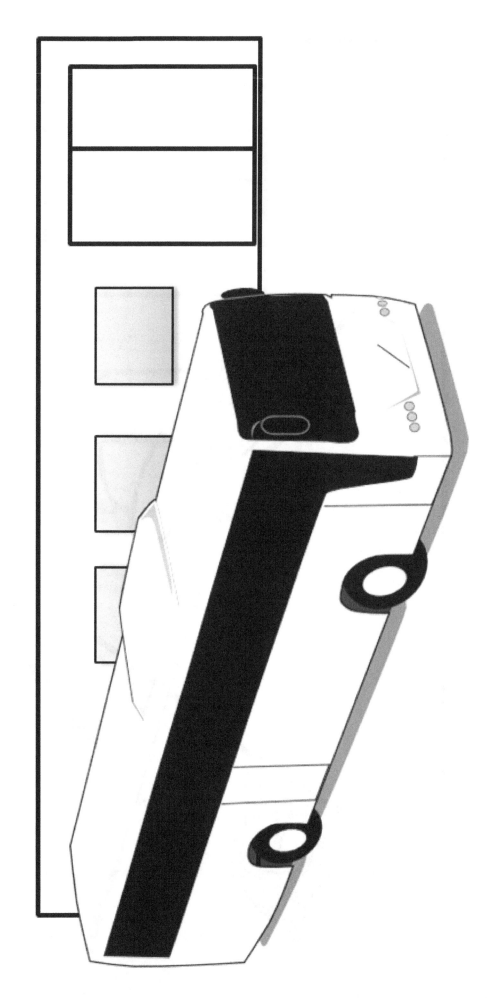

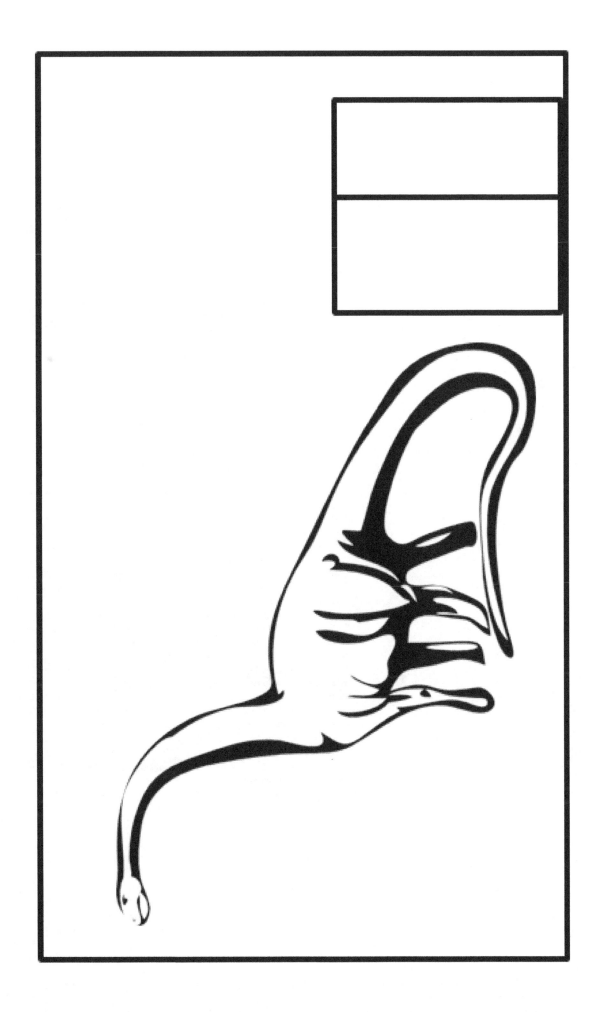

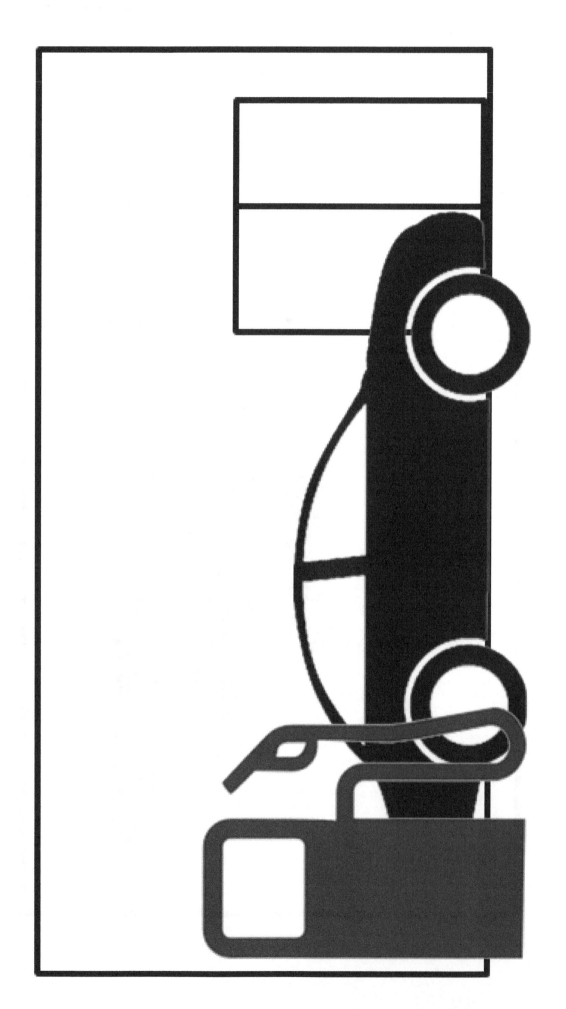

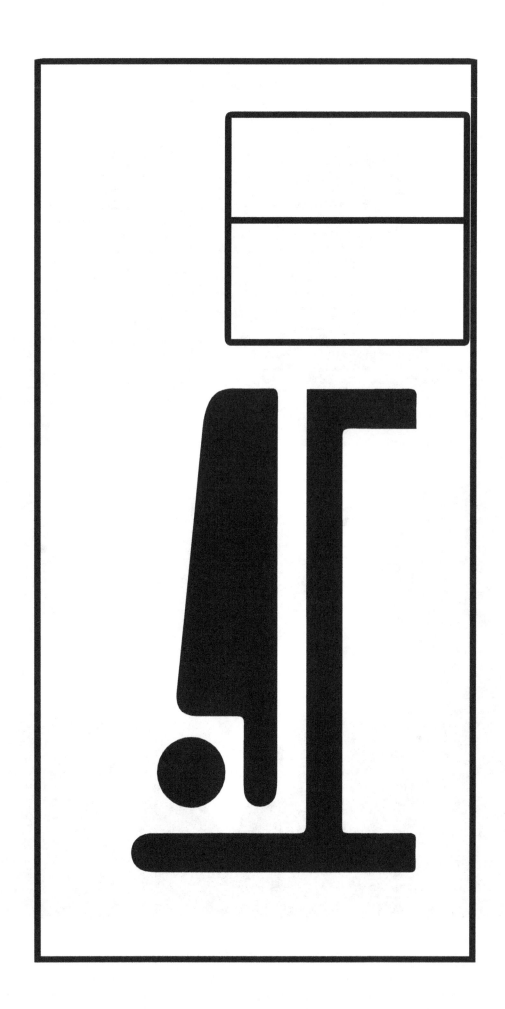

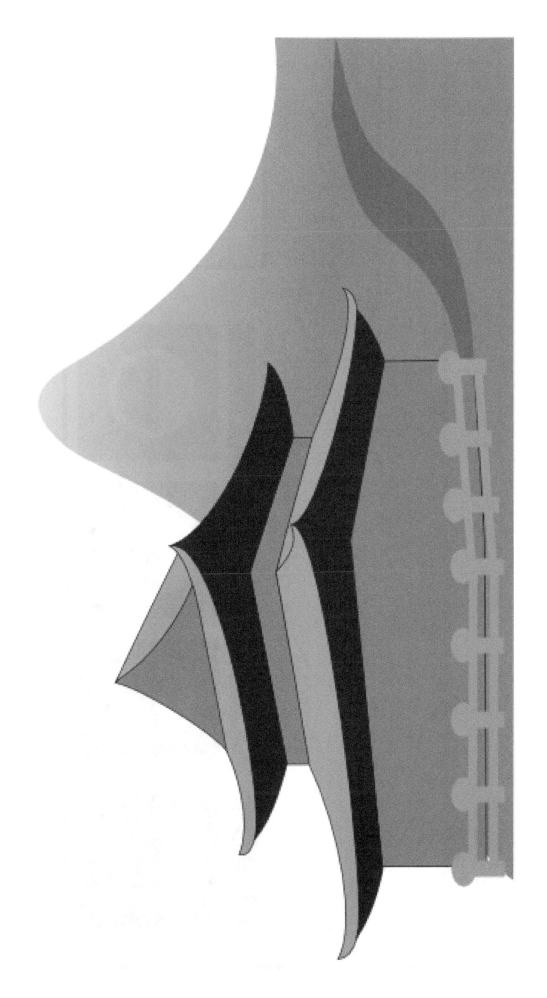

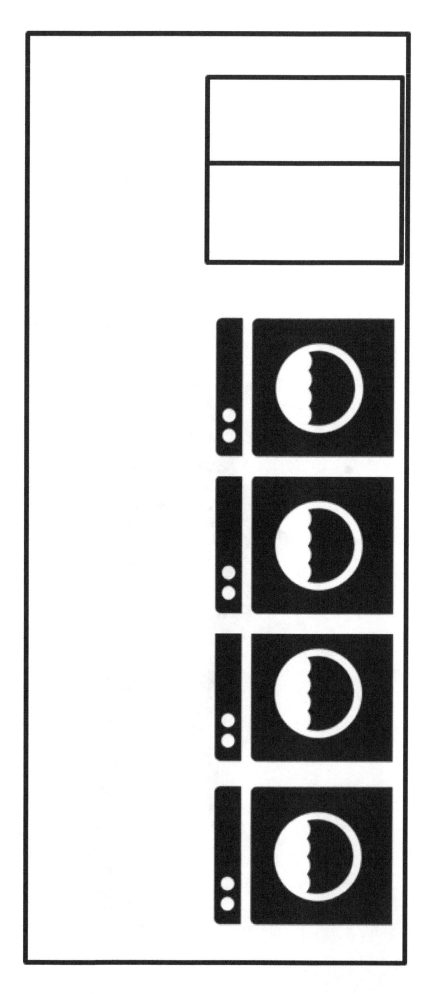

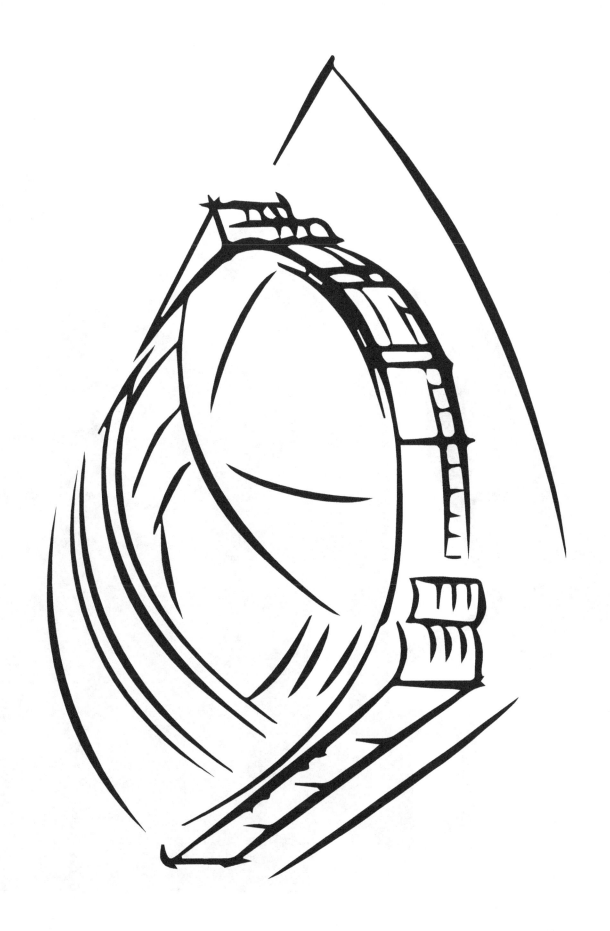

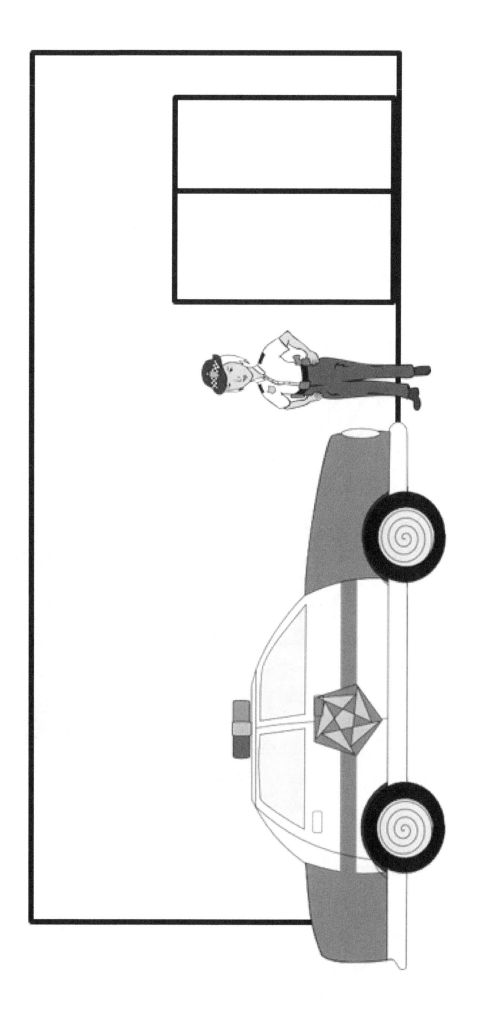

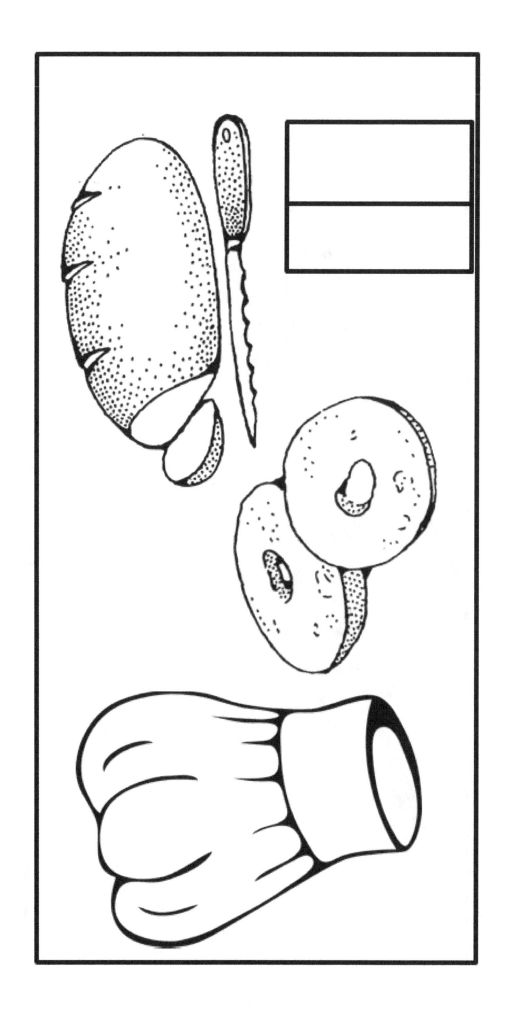

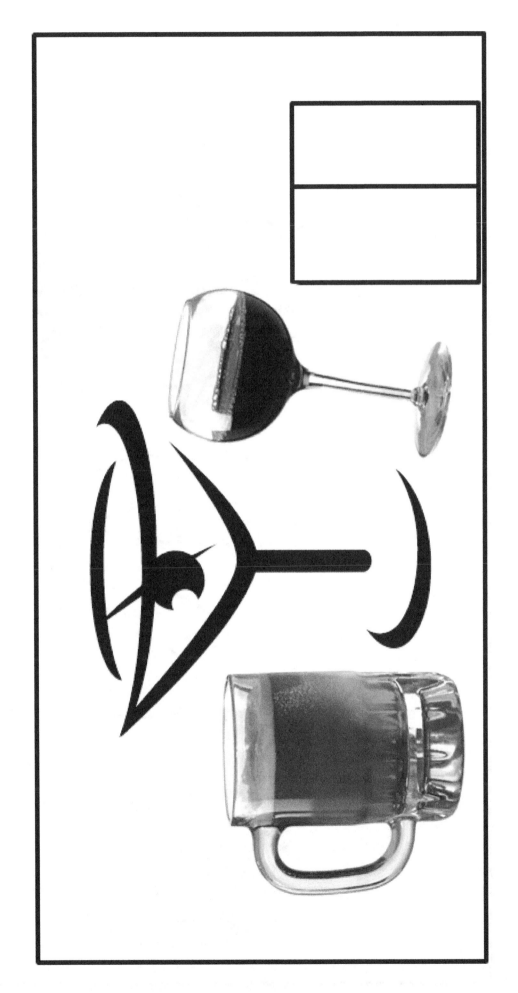

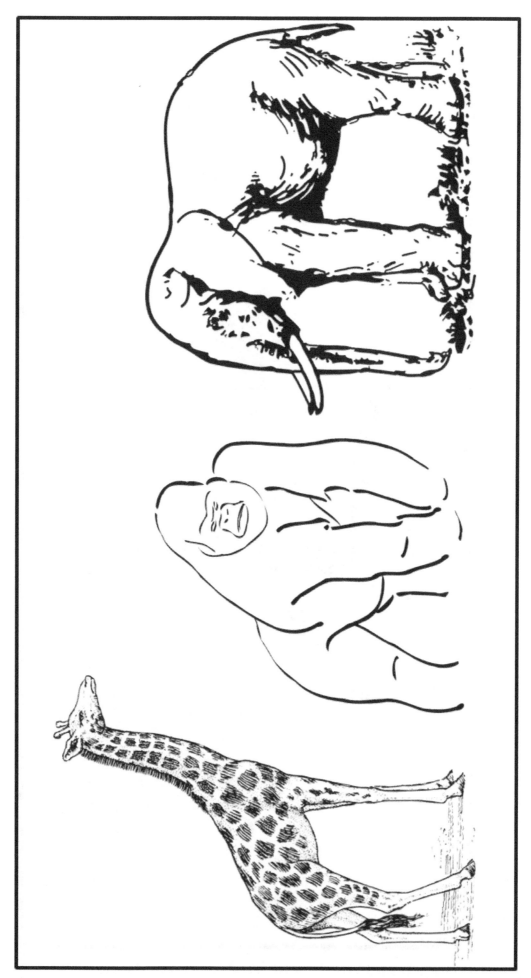

Bingo Cards

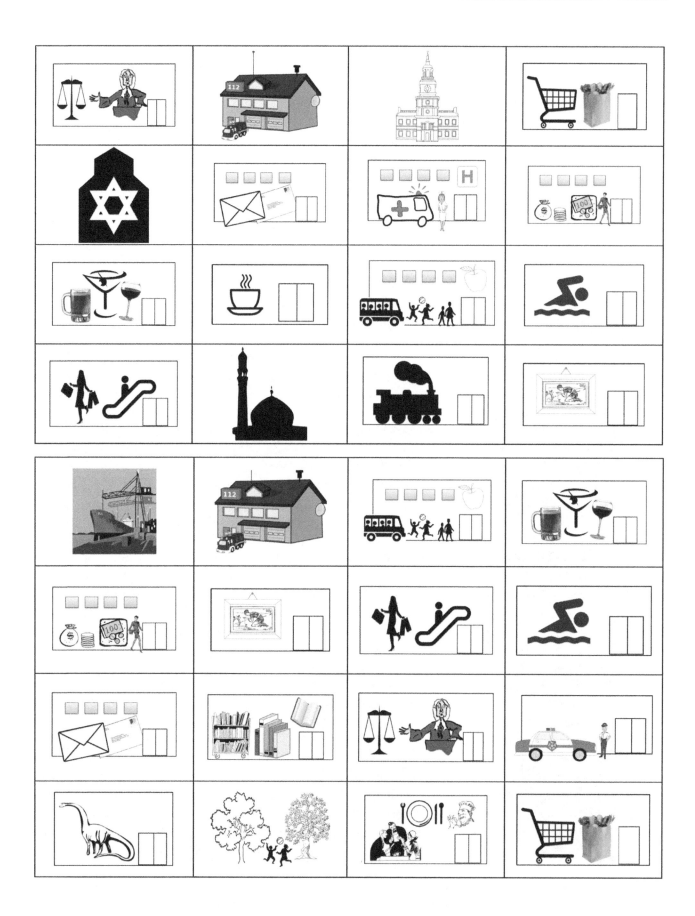

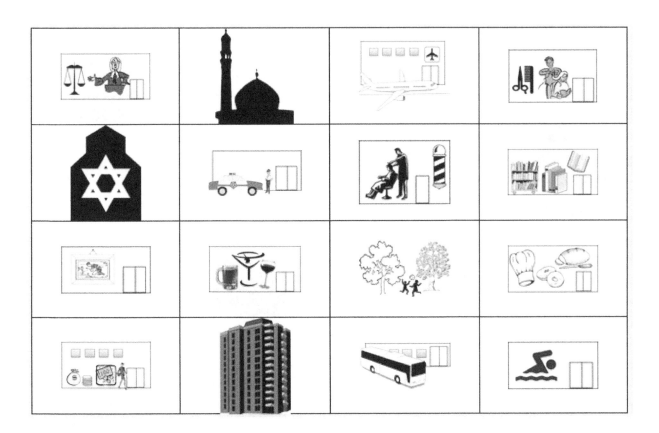

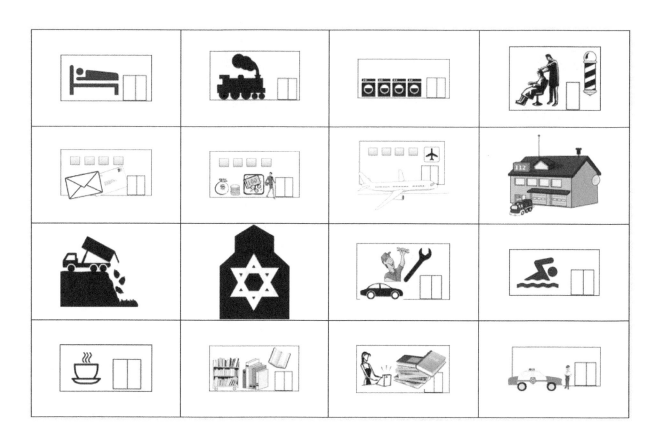

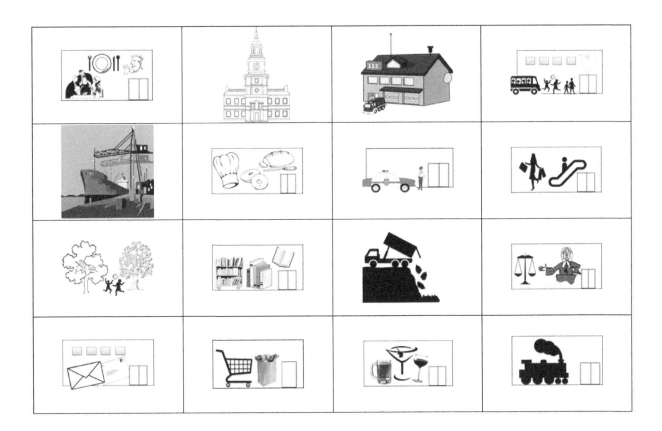

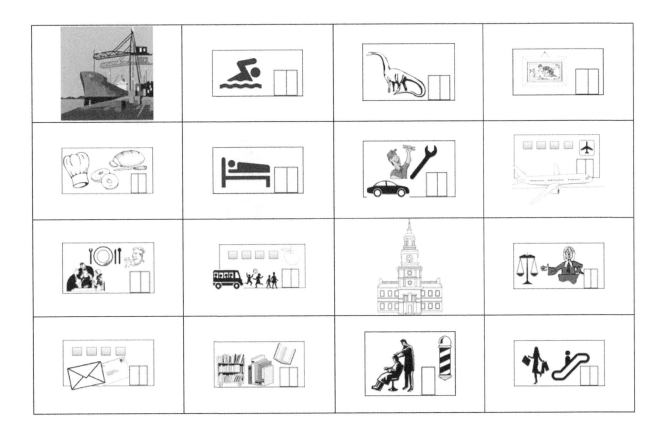

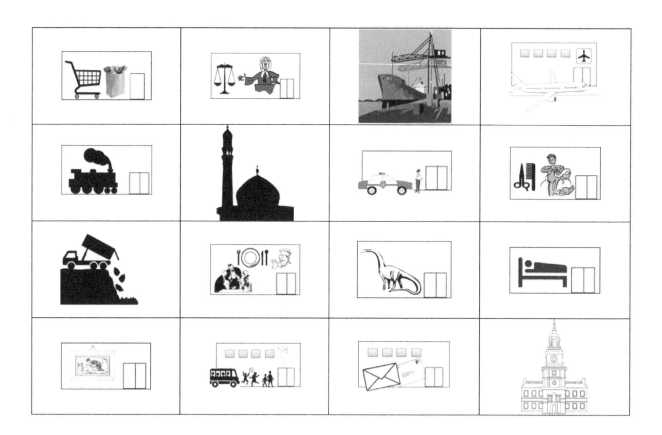

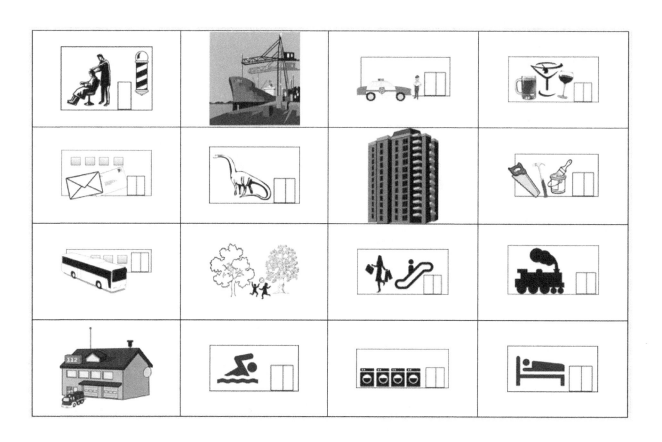

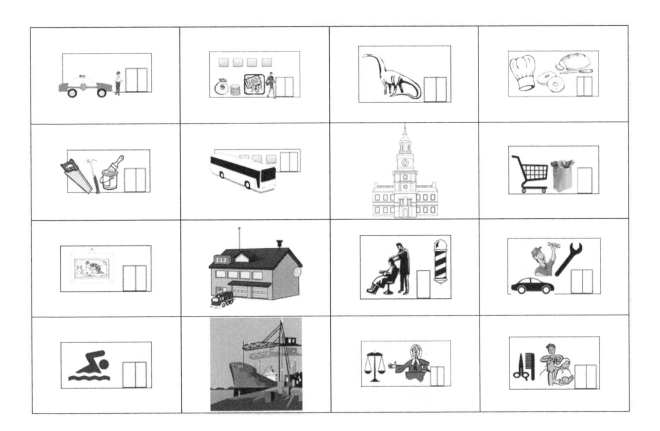

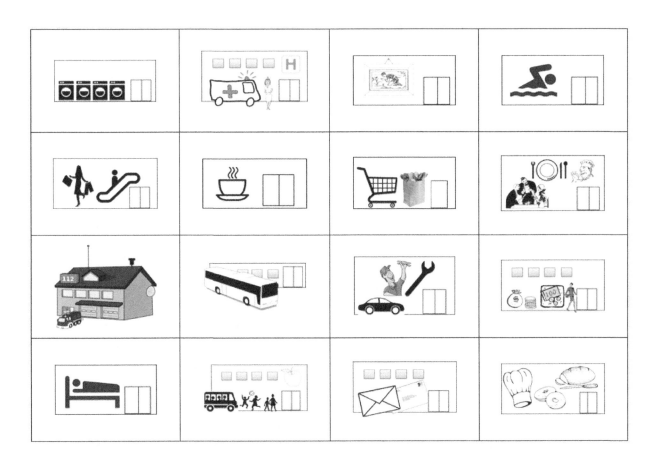

Made in United States
Orlando, FL
04 August 2023

35784372R00076